This is a limited collector's edition.

SOURCE OF THE RIVER

poems by

Deborah Fleming

Finishing Line Press
Georgetown, Kentucky

SOURCE OF THE RIVER

Copyright © 2018 by Deborah Fleming
ISBN 978-1-63534-413-4 First Edition
All rights reserved under International and Pan-American Copyright Conventions.
No part of this book may be reproduced in any manner whatsoever without written permission from the publisher, except in the case of brief quotations embodied in critical articles and reviews.

ACKNOWLEDGMENTS

Some of the poems in this volume were originally published in the following journals:

Amaryllis Review: "John Hanning Speke at the Shore of Victoria-Nyanza" and "John Hanning Speke at the Ripon Falls"

Green River Review: "Atkins Hamerton at Zanzibar"

Pennsylvania Review: "Bagamoyo"

Yet Another Small Magazine: "The Falls of Panga-Ní"

Publisher: Leah Maines

Editor: Christen Kincaid

Cover Art: http://wikimedia.com/

Author Photo: courtesy of author

Cover Design: Elizabeth Maines McCleavy

Printed in the USA on acid-free paper.
Order online: www.finishinglinepress.com
　　　　　also available on amazon.com

　　　　　　　　Author inquiries and mail orders:
　　　　　　　　　　Finishing Line Press
　　　　　　　　　　　P. O. Box 1626
　　　　　　　　　Georgetown, Kentucky 40324
　　　　　　　　　　　　U. S. A.

Table of Contents

Isak Dinesen in Denmark 1

Colonel John May on His Journey to the Ohio Country, 1788 3

Kumari 8

Source of the River

    Atkins Hamerton at Zanzibar 13

    Sir Richard Burton Approaching Zanzibar by Night 15

    Pemba 17

    Mombasa 19

    Bagamoyo 20

    The Journey Inland 21

    John Hanning Speke at the Shore of Victoria-Nyanza 23

    John Hanning Speke at the Ripon Falls 24

    The Falls of Panga-Ní 25

Notes

About the Author

For Edward Lense

Isak Dinesen in Denmark

Have I lived only once that I am so many?

My father stayed among the Cree in north
Wisconsin, on the frozen shores of lakes
that have no name in English; traveled
the rim of Asia and rode downriver in the Congo.
My brother followed in his footsteps,
writer and explorer, while I set sail for Africa
and carved a farm on hills above Nairobi
whose dusty streets became to me
the center of the earth.

I rode across the tawny lion-haunted
plains where elephants, those great gray boulders,
rolled, and crested cranes called out clear notes
like church bells ringing from the treetops;
flamingoes, proud waders of the Nile,
sisters to the lotus, floated, sunset-clouds
above the land, the curve of neck and bill
so self-possessed like gracious ladies
in their gaudy plumes while vast snow fields
of Kilimanjaro shimmered in the sun.

Somalis told me stories of magic horses
living in the river-bottom that rose at full moon-time
from oozy currents to mate with mares
and breed the foals of greatest swiftness.

Now returned to this, my flat and frozen landscape
hemmed in by sea and sky, in this great house
where ghosts still tread the hallways, I write their
stories through the clear resounding bell of allegory,

though Europe marched across its borders,
and my losses faded in the mud
and death of millions.

Must we be forever separate from what we love
to know we love it? Can we never look the present
in the face? Where now the call of crested crane,
those beautiful flamingoes dancing in the river shallows?
Why can we never finally return?

Colonel John May on His Journey to the Ohio Country, 1788

       June
I must rise before my men
if ever I desire to write,
for when they see me thus,
they not unjustly think me idle.

Weeks ago we crossed the mountains
that separate the world of Christians
from that of savages. Five strong,
we lodged at Pittsburgh where at evening
on the deck I watched the sun descend
into the meeting-place of rivers Huron call
Monongehela, Allegheny, from whence
the clear and mighty one flows south
and west. The people here are lazy,
for the woods are full of fruit, and every
throw into the current brings forth
a brimming net of fish.

At Bethlehem John Heckewelder greeted us–
a man renowned for saving souls–invited us
to meeting and to dinner on the ground.
Like many who have lived too long among
these savages, he claims they're persons
just like Christians, lauds them for their courage
and their hunting. His good woman too forever
praises savage women's cooking and their ways
of raising children–never beating them
nor rating them in any way, and saying that
the young men and their squaws grow straight
and brave, and face all consequences with
a stoic grace–with so much generosity
you'd swear she wasn't in her wits.

We followed the Ohio south to Marietta
where we met with Clark and with Saint Clair

to learn the terms of treaty they had struck
with certain chiefs at Fort Finney on the Big Miami.
Kímtony had signed, and now the land is safe
from the river to the north, and we may pass
unhindered to the place whereto I wend my way
into the west.

The people here are superstitious,
being French; they tied a leg of mutton
to a pole which they held above the water;
where it dipped, they said, the body
of a drowned man would be found.

      July
From that place we followed the Muskingum
northward and were plagued by thunder-gusts
and howling winds. Naught surrounded us
but groaning trees, and we were soaked
and pelted by unceasing rain. Next day we rode
upriver. Hills and valleys rose progressively
to view, and though I try with all my learning
in the tongue of Christian men I cannot
do it justice–it would take a poet's pen to tell
these beauties–blue hills beyond blue hills.

At last we came into the country
where the river bends toward the west,
where wild flowers decorate a meadow
in the midst of giant forest groves,
where wild men and creatures sported
in the days before we brought true word
and industry. Indeed, I think I know
the reason they have not progressed
in like manner to the Europeans, for who
would toil when the woods provide for all,
their clothes and houses being simple
like themselves?

On Wednesday last we laid our axes
to the ancient tenants of the wood.
This land is good as any that I've seen
and will reward industrious men,
watered as it is by frequent showers
and the generous dews of heaven.
Here I will build a western outpost
as I prospect for gain and wish to leave
my name upon a town land.

One man's hands were broken when a tree limb
fell on him. We sent him back to Marietta,
for we cannot feed a man who cannot work.
Yet we never lack for food: this day but one
my hunter killed a buffalo, five deer,
one timber wolf, three turkeys.

      August
Three of us rode northward where I slept
and dreamt I sailed eastward from our home
in Boston and was overcome by seas
that heaved and bellowed like to Jonah's whale,
then woke to pelting rain and winds that swayed
the biggest trees. In consequence, I have an illness
that will not relent.

We stocked ourselves with furs and fruit,
raccoon, deer, bear, and ginseng root
and headed back. We lost a pack horse
and its cargo at a swollen stream.
Also, the rider drowned. Now we are two
and must appear like Quixote and his Sancho
tilting at a statue.

Unto Muskingum we returned to find
my lodge burned down, the sentry knifed,
no doubt by savages who still ignore

the treaty. The forest is already claiming
fields we cleared two months ago. My men
set fire to this section of the wood
to warn the perpetrators. But my western
outpost is no more. We turned our faces
to the east again, at Marietta sold our cargo
to the settlers so as to ride unburdened homeward.

    September
My men were picking wild berries to stew
with meat and so I walked into the wood
and stood beside a pond wherein the fish
were leaping. I thought one time I heard
them speak, and saw a heron standing there,
its long neck like a shepherd's crook. I trespass
here who look upon the noble creature, dreaming
of my life in Boston, lost ambition, years
that I spent planning when I could have lived
as solitary, self-possessed just like this statue-
figure on his long and slender legs.

My men have followed me, I know not why,
since they can earn as much from anyone,
but do my bidding, work with honesty
and cheer through all these trials we have faced.

Where I step I crush the grass; where I
ride the grasses part but flow back in
when I have gone as if I am a passing
frigate that upon the ocean plows a path
and leaves behind smooth water, yet no trace
remains when wind and tide erase again
the sea-track. So we turn and face the sunrise
once again.

At Bethlehem the choir women all in white
appeared like saints disburdened of this earth.

What though the heathen rage, and savage nations roar and yell in midnight hellish revels? We shall not be moved. Our feet stand fast upon the earth, our bow is bent in strength, our arms enforced by Jacob's God. This land is ours. The fullness thereof wishes us to prosper and subdue.

Kumari

1. Kumari Bahal, Kathmandu

Behind the white stucco facade,
entrance guarded by lions made of stone,
you cross a cobbled courtyard, pass
high pottery jars that hold
wide-spreading ferns surrounded
by gates of iron. Brick walls
rise to a red-tiled roof.

Opposite, pillars support
a shadowed walkway,
pointed arches framing three
dark windows intricately carved,
fine latticework on windows
along the sides, reaching outward
like a crown, lintels carved with skulls
laughing either at life or death,
hewn lesser deities, peacocks, doves,
adorn the stately balconies above.
A notice reads: No Foreigners
Beyond This Point. No
Photographs.

Behind white curtains partly
drawn, the virgin Kanya Kumari,
also called Parvati, Shiva's *shakti*,
paces rooms of the sacred *bahal*,
not a vestal but a living spirit,
Dorga–Ashta Matrika,
Mother-of-All–yet pure,
chosen from the Sakya clan–
those who work in gold and silver–
the Hindu Living Goddess,
worshiped also by the Buddhists,
for the flawlessness of eyes,
skin, arms, hands; even her stars

must with the king's be aligned.
Her feet may never touch the earth
because she is a thing apart,
and to look upon her often
is an act of sacrilege.

2. Newar Valley (12th Century)

The Malla king, bored with wealth
inside a kingdom ringed with
shrouded Himalayan peaks,
played dice with goddess Teleju,
who came to him in human form
when she heard his sigh of boredom.
He soon lusted after her,
but she refused his importunities,
and disappeared among the mountain mists,
whereupon he begged her to return,
prayed day and night, promised
he would lust no more. Teleju,
moved at last by pity of his prayer,
gave him the Kumari, said to him,
"In her I am found; worship her,
in a maiden recognize the goddess,
but keep her well away from prying
eyes, just out of reach, for men
cannot often look upon the god
or goddess, but now and then
reveal her flawless face, for even
faith must be replenished, the miracle
must at times be witnessed,
men must drink at the ever-flowing
fountain, lest they forget. Do not
allow her feet to touch the ground,
for though she lives, she must be found
pure and undefiled as well as beautiful."

3. Durbar Square, Kathmandu

Beyond the tables of bright-colored cloth
and vendors selling fruit and herbs,
wool, string, pottery, and beads, dark
Temple Teleju rises layer upon layer.
Black goats are tethered by the neck
to be given her as sacrifice,
temples garlanded in silk. Two stone
lions at the Khoka Hanuman
are ridden by the Shiva, the other
by his *shakti,* Parvati, and by Krishna,
God of Love, incarnation in this world
of Vishnu, god of gods, preserver, creator,
and destroyer. Sun illuminates the streets
but pilgrims walk inside abodes of gods
who must always hide themselves
and never gaze upon the sun.

4. Chaldang Gompa

My family gave me up
to be the goddess at the age of five,
to personify both fruitfulness and purity
when I still played with dolls,
long before I understood
perfection of the living body,
to walk here and to let them
dress me in golden robes
with pearl embroideries, my hair
enwound with silver cords,
my crown inlaid with emeralds.
All teaching was denied to me
while my brothers went to school,
as goddesses possess no need of learning.
I was taken out to festivals
when I rode upon an elephant

through the thronged and garlanded
streets of Kathmandu. When I reached
my gush of blood and pain that rips
the body through,
they gave me back to him,
my father whom I never really knew,
who then arranged a match,
and at the age of twelve
I was married to a farmer.
These from whom I had god-power
declared that now I was a common woman,
who steps bare-foot upon the dust,
cooks food, spins cloth, gathers firewood,
draws water, sweeps floors,
milks goats, bears children,
and worships now at Shiva's shrine.
This man my husband
slaughters a goat outside the door.
Then he orders me to bed,
and I, a goddess once, obey.
His mother laughs at me,
twice replaced by goddesses
of recent coin. Ten years now
I've been his wife, and I must find
my happiness in my lost beauty,
and on the lower hillside gaze
at the mountain rising in the mist,
the water plunging from the crags,
towering snow-draped peaks,
the buffalo that slowly draws the plough,
the sheep that graze, the cries of children
playing as I never had a chance to do.
I dwell among the people
who chose me, worshiped me,
then cast me out to walk the roads.

At last I saw Parvati goddess
is all women; youth and beauty
are their emblem, for they all
have once been young, and all
for beauty strive. All mothers
once were virgins, and in their bearing
bring forth a new beginning
even as their menfolk
strive in loving to attain the goddess–
though they see her every morning
through the haze of their own dreaming.

The miracle is this: In me the gods
have given back themselves as all
the gods are worshiped, brought low,
and exalted once again with every birth.
I work and know I was a goddess once,
who now must walk upon the earth.

Source of the River

Atkins Hamerton at Zanzibar

27 June 1857

I dreamt last evening
that we stood again at Menai Bay, my friend,
looking across the mangrove swamp to Kwale.
I saw the Persian Zizimkazi mosque
saved by Kiza's prayers and a swarm of bees.
Then from a hill above the town
we gazed on slope-roofed huts
of Tumbatu and Hadima, merchants' palaces
turned scarlet by the setting sun,
dry creek bed where at low tide
we raced our horses.

I was alone then. The horse had carried
you away, and I saw Zanzibar the way
it used to be, the Arab *dhows* swept inland
by *mvuli*, red-tiled roofs, white walls
of coral stone with long verandas
and dark balustrades, carved Indian
doorways looking out on narrow alleys,
great fig trees with aerial roots like columns.

Prostitutes with faces like skinned apes
and long, lean legs in red silk tights
strode the wider boulevards; I heard
a screaming Circassian dragged by his ankles
in the chains, heard cracking bones
and saw a dog tearing a dead slave.
I remember sometimes fifty bodies
thrown upon that beach. At least,
my friend, we put a stop to that.

They still come, your Highness,
the caravans, often a thousand strong,

from Abyssinia and Somaliland.
Fifty years you were the sultan here
and could not stop it. And Palmerston:
"The Arabs should betake themselves
to cultivation of the soil

and to commerce that is innocent."
That we could end with royal wish
the custom of nine hundred years!
It was too heavy a stone to lift.

I think of tall areca groves
that grow beside the stream
all green and blue like County Wicklow.
These last two weeks I've dreamt
so much of home, and rain that draws
a veil across the valley like a seine.

Now surf is pounding up the strand
like hooves of horses racing on the sand.

Sir Richard Burton Approaching Zanzibar by Night

1857

Waves lapping at the bow, we drifted
toward the shore. Beaches sparkled
with glow-worms and flitting fire-flies.

Burning leaves and grass
illuminated shallow pools where
tribesmen speared their fish.

Torches in canoes on crimpled water
scattered in a blaze of light;
on the smooth, the flare became

a trembling pyramid. In the Bazaar
lines of Negroes stood like beasts–
the sick ones squatted–ribs protruding

like the girders of a cask. The broker
shouted, cracked his whip. Dogs
slunk about with lolling tongues.

A leather-skinned Mauritian
had crucified some rebel slaves
because the sun was hot one day,

nailed their feet fast to the deck,
hands to capstan bars,
lashed some across the masts.

Teeth gripping his cigar,
he bragged his story on the dock
above the black and trembling tide.

I saw smoking blood, a red-hot poker
drawn across the grasslands and the jungles

which rose before me on that darkened flood

under screams of early gulls.

Pemba

Sir Richard Burton, 1862

From Kokoto-Ni for three days
we stumbled at a single knot an hour
in the old tub, her mast
loose like a slaver's.
High winds forced down sail;
our watchman suffered
with the squalls.

A dome of hills like solid air,
torched by sunlight,
embraced the coast.
Green mangroves edged
the crystal sand and calabash
stretched crooked arms
above the clustered huts.
Their girths of forty feet and more
exceed the trees of Solomon.

No wind ruffled graceful palms
that stood like living columns;
convolvuli were closing yellow
eyes upon our coming.

Some trees were bare,
others in bud, leaf, or blossom,
so that all seasons tarried there
at once. The river here called
Rovuma lay still and green, yet flowed;
trees drooped from beds of corraline
above the seas now verdigris, now blue,
depending on the point of view.

We crossed a tidal-drained lagoon
that kept the castle safe,
walked miles over crab mounds

before we saw the fort
raised by Portuguese invaders
from the stones of Persian walls.
Ruined towers rose above the vines,
every stone precipitous
and crumbling.

Spars of Arab slave-ships,
like jousting spears,
peered through curtained trees.

Mombasa

Sir Richard Burton, 1862

The broken line of wooded hills,
the Rabai Range, rises behind the town;
purple during storms and evenings,
they are hazy blue at noon time.

During drought, Arab merchants
race their horses in the creek beds.
Daring riders, in full stride
they lean to catch up stones.

The native Wamasai, nomads tall and dark,
shelter under skins but build no huts.
They live for stealing cattle, gift of gods
and right of strength.

Bees are sacred. Mkámba's legend
says that he attacked a hive
and lived to see his cattle
changed to buffalo and antelope.

Oratory rages like a storm;
every limb participates in speech.
The cymbals and the drums are never silent,
sweeping trees, plains, mountains

into frenzied pounding when the tribes
attack or when a man approaches death.
Funerals are great festivities:
bodies hurl themselves in arcs

around the fire. The sober chieftain
booms out: "He is ended."
They bury dead beneath the hills
and have no afterlife.

Bagamoyo

Sir Richard Burton, 1862

Waving coconut palms line the shore.
Behind them leaves blaze scarlet,
lean longingly across the bay.
The ancient coral mosque at Kaole
shone amber in the setting sun
when we rode past.

Beyond the slope, a caravan
arrives from Unyamezi, garden
of the plains of Tanganyika. Women
trudge in single file, many hundred,
hands and arms secured to poles,
mouths twisted in their agony.
Faces hidden in their hoods,
the slavers follow, cracking whips.

Nyamwezi guide the Arabs
to the camps of enemies–
Rwandans, Congolese.
They shoot the men as they awake,
cut off hands and fingers
for bracelets and for copper rings.

Sea foam scatters on the reef.
Sails at Bagamoyo harbor
flutter in the wind
like empty sleeves.

The Journey Inland

John Hanning Speke, 6 January 1858

"Why do you leave your friends so soon?"
asked Said Bin Salim. "A shooting expedition
on the Rufu," I answered him.
"Why do you take no Diwan guide?"
he asked, as if he knew. "We go
in secret," I rejoined, but thought,
we want no spies. We hired a long canoe
and oarsmen, started with the tide.

We resolved to visit Chogwe–
where even slavers never sail
because the jungle there is dark–
and then to push for Fuga
and the Falls of Panga-Ní.

At the river's mouth a gale
drove us up the stream. Sun
glimmered through the canopy
of bombax trees with buttressed
shafts; lianas hung like rigging
from the boughs. Monkeys
swung on bush-ropes. Crocodiles
swaggered, eyes glinting at us
under warty brows. By noon
the river narrowed, no longer
white with surging over rocks
but clear as any Zangian lake.
A paddy-hopper darted here and there.
Fish sprang into the air,
throwing light like silver plates.
Oysters clung to mangrove roots
denuded by the tides. Gnomish baobob trees
clicked their knobbled fingers.
Doves cooed in denser leaves.

Evening wrapped its haze around us.
Beasts roared fitfully. Treetops
and the gurgling stream drowned
the oarsmen's calls. Leaves like human
palms outstretched were gray,
no longer green. I saw Said's unbelieving
eyes. "You shall find your
destination," his last words to me.

The soul comes here for rest,
desires nearness to decay–
no autumn, only bloom and death.

Branches dropped away. The oarsmen
steered no longer. No one spoke,
no more thought of Zanzibar.
The river flowed a sable streak,
an avenue dividing lofty sentinels,
that conveyed us to the heart of earth.

Stars gleamed like lamps in limpid air.
Fireflies rose in a shower of sparks,
bright worlds that spin into the void
and disappear.

John Hanning Speke at the Shore of Victoria-Nyanza

3 August 1858

At last I am here. The first white man
to see it all–the junction of two hemispheres,
the father of rivers, and its mother, Nyanza,
the Buganda call it. I name it Victoria.

Near Mwanza the lake itself breaks into view,
the lake the Kazeh Arabs say
is greater than the Tanganyika.
Marenga trees traverse the slopes
to meet the yellow sands,
and hippos like dark river-gods
lumber at the water's edge.

My guides are drinking plantain wine.

Here at the southern end the water runs
between the grassy banks, festooned
with lilac convolvuli and white acacias,
and is impeded by a natural dam
where it forms a kind of garden-pond,
though black and still.

Across the stream a wooded islet
rises from the lake where
on a moonlit night
the savages might meet to play
some dark and dreadful tragedy.

John Hanning Speke
at the Ripon Falls

28 July 1862

Like a tidal wave the great stream
pours itself into the river.
Fish leap into the falls. Wasoga
and Waganda fishermen
paddle in a line across the lake.
I should baptize myself
like Moses.

I alone accomplished this journey,
calculated the river's altitude,
established the Nile's source.
It stretches thirty-four degrees of latitude,
one eleventh of the distance
round the earth.

At Ngambési King Mtése told me
that Nyanza is a god that
rises in tremendous storms,
tears up islands and carries them away.
He asked why I pursued the river, asked,
if I found it, would my people
make me a god? I told him yes.

There seems no end to this vast sheet
of water. More like the sea, it takes
the colour of the skies, blue on fairest days,
grey on cloudy ones. Lake and sky at sunset
burst in flaming light. Waves
crackle on the reeds, and,
in the deepening night,
the lily trotters and the ibis send
continual inharmonious cries.

The Falls of Panga Ní

John Hanning Speke, 1862

Opal-tinted mists floated
on the blue-gray depths.
Curling smoke wreaths
foretold a storm. Coral
cloud light strayed upon
the Fugan highlands'
rounded cones, green and
terra-cotta. Copper mountains
creased themselves in rugged
folds above gazelle-grazed
meadows. The falling water
thunders over boulders,
rises higher than the trees.

My bearers chant into the evening,
singing loneliness away, as the sunset
turns the lake to golden fire,
source of the Nile, who gave life
to Nephirtiti worshiping her Atwan–
god of sun and river, whose consort
is the lake. Ibis cry and float above her.

Although she wrote the legends
into land where men are wild
as gazelles, where she spreads
her silted cape she birthed
the highest culture known to man.

How far must I journey
to step into the same river twice?
She has found me orphaned
and alone. My song is the song
of the wind, my cry that of the ibis,
my heart the heart of the lake,
source of the everlasting river.

Notes

Isak Dinesen in Denmark: Isak Dinesen, pen name of Baroness Karen Blixen, was nominated for the Nobel Prize in 1961 and was a friend of Ernest Hemingway and Igor Stravinsky.

Col. John May on His Journey to the Ohio Country: Col. John May made two trips to the Ohio Country in the 18th Century. John Heckewelder was a missionary to the Shawnee and other native people.

Source of the River: Most of the details in these poems are taken from John Hanning Speke, *Journal of the Discovery of the Source of the Nile* (1868), and Sir Richard Burton, *The Nile Basin* (1864) and *Zanzibar: City, Island, and Coast* (1872).

Atkins Hamerton at Zanzibar: Atkins Hamerton was British consul to Zanzibar from 1841 until his death in 1857. Palmerston was British Prime Minister at the time. Hamerton and his friend Seyyid Said bin Sultan, who preceded Hamerton in death, tried unsuccessfully to curtail the slave trade through Zanzibar Island. The reference to Kiza and the Persian mosque comes from a folk tale. *Mvuli* are ocean storms. *Dhows* are small sailing vessels.

Sir Richard Burton Approaching Zanzibar by Night: Sir Richard Burton, a British explorer in search of the source of the Nile, arrived in 1857 at Zanzibar Island, center of the Arab slave trade.

Pemba: Pemba is an island north of Zanzibar in the Indian Ocean. The Persian ruins date from the 12th Century, the Portuguese ones from the 17th.

Bagamoyo: "Bagamoyo" means "lay down the burden of your heart."

By the same author

Poetry
Into a New Country
Morning, Winter Solstice
Migrations

Fiction
Without Leave

Scholarly Editions
Towers of Myth and Stone: Yeats's Influence on Robinson Jeffers
"A man who does not exist": The Irish Peasant in the Work of W. B. Yeats and J. M. Synge

Edited Collections
W. B. Yeats and Postcolonialism
Learning the Trade: W. B. Yeats and Contemporary Poetry

Deborah Fleming is author of two previous collections of poems, *Morning, Winter Solstice* (2012) and *Into a New Country* (2016), as well as a chapbook, *Migrations* (2005), and a novel, *Without Leave* (2014), winner of the Asheville Award from Black Mountain Press. She has also published *"A man who does not exist": The Irish Peasant in the Work of W. B. Yeats and J. M. Synge* (1995), *Towers of Myth and Stone: Yeats's Influence on Robinson Jeffers* (2015), *W. B. Yeats and Postcolonialism* (2000), and *Learning the Trade: W. B. Yeats and Contemporary Poetry* (1992) as well as articles on Yeats, Jeffers, Eamon Grennan, and Aldo Leopold. Four of her poems have been nominated for the Pushcart Prize. Winner of a Vandewater Poetry Award and grants from the National Endowment for the Humanities and National Council of Learned Societies, she is director and editor of the Ashland Poetry Press. Currently she lives on a farm in northeast Ohio.

www.ingramcontent.com/pod-product-compliance
Lightning Source LLC
LaVergne TN
LVHW041513070426
835507LV00012B/1542